ISLE OF MAN

TRAVEL GUIDE

2024

A definitive guide to explore the unrivaled Beauty , ageless attraction, enrichment, and unmatched adventure in UK.

Kenneth Finley

Copyright

TABLE OF CONTENTS

ABOUT THIS GUIDE

This thorough travel guide to the alluring Isle of Man has been painstakingly chosen to be the perfect travel companion in 2024. This book is intended to enrich your travel by offering a seamless combination of important information and local knowledge. It includes a wealth of insightful information and personal experiences. This guide's goal is to uncover the hidden treasures and reveal the intricate tapestry of the Isle of Man's distinctive offers with an emphasis on experiential exploration and cultural immersion.

Benefits:

- **In-Depth Local Knowledge**: This book gives a nuanced view of the Isle of Man's unique geography, cultural legacy, and lively community, enabling you to dig deeper into its essence. It is supported by the knowledge of seasoned travelers and local insiders.

- **Customized Itineraries**: Whether you have a week or more to spare, customized itineraries for a range of lengths enable you to make the most of your time and fully enjoy the many delights of the Isle of Man.

- **Exclusive Insights into Hidden Gems:** Discover the Isle of Man's well-kept secrets, from remote settlements tucked away in verdant hills to off-the-beaten-path treks giving spectacular vistas, to ensure you come upon the island's best-kept secrets.

- **Up-to-Date Information**: Keep up-to-date with new developments, forthcoming activities, and freshly opened attractions so you can take advantage of every chance to interact with the Isle of Man's changing environment and vibrant cultural scene.

- **Practical Trip Advice**: This book provides you with invaluable guidance to explore the island flawlessly, providing a hassle-free and rewarding trip experience. It covers everything from visa procedures and packing needs to local etiquette and safety standards.

- **Cultural Immersion & Experiences:** Develop a strong connection to the Isle of Man's rich cultural history by immersing yourself in the island's lively customs, indulging in its mouth watering regional food, and taking part in its dynamic festivals and events.

- **Insider Tips**: Get insider advice on the top restaurants, genuine lodgings, and interesting gift stores so you may experience the true flavor of the Isle of Man and make treasured memories that will last a lifetime.

Your key to the Isle of Man's unrivaled beauty and ageless attraction, this travel book will ensure that every minute of your visit is filled with discovery, enrichment, and unmatched adventure.

1. INTRODUCTION TO THE ISLE OF MAN

1.1. About the Isle of Man

The Isle of Man, which is nestled in the Irish Sea between Great Britain and Ireland, emits a special charm because of its spectacular natural surroundings and rich cultural legacy. This self-governing British Crown Dependency, which has a land area of around 572 square kilometers, has a populace renowned for its kind hospitality and lively customs. The ancient structures, medieval castles, and historical sites on the island are evidence of the island's long history. The Isle of Man's moderate marine climate, which has cold winters and warm summers, makes it an ideal location for year-round exploration.

Visitors looking for a break from the hustle and bustle of city life are drawn to the island's rough coastline, which is studded with magnificent cliffs and sandy bays. Beyond its natural beauty, the Isle of Man has a special appeal for adventure seekers because of its famous motorsport competitions, such as the thrilling Isle of Man TT races, which draw daredevils and racing fanatics from all over the world. The Isle of Man, which embodies a compelling combination of traditional and modern elements, ensures that everyone who travels to its beaches will have an unforgettable and varied travel experience.

1.2. Why Visit in 2024?

1.2.1 Exciting Events and Festivals: 2024 is expected to be filled with a wide range of exciting events and festivals that will highlight the island's cultural diversity and artistic energy. Each event offers a fascinating immersion into the island's vibrant customs and energetic community spirit, from the Isle of Man TT races that give the island an unmatched vitality to the spectacular Tynwald Day festivities honoring the island's legislative past.

1.2.2 Unspoiled Natural Beauty: The Isle of Man is a haven for those who like the outdoors and tranquilly, providing pristine landscapes and quiet seascapes. 2024 offers the ideal opportunity to immerse oneself in the island's unspoiled natural splendor, establishing a deep connection with its breathtaking surroundings. Its expansive vegetation, meandering walking routes, and panoramic panoramas.

1.2.3 Rich Historical Exploration: The Isle of Man's fascinating past may be uncovered by history buffs in 2024 thanks to the island's abundance of protected historical monuments and landmarks. Each historical monument acts as a portal to the island's enthralling history, enabling visitors to embark on an immersive trip through time, from the majestic castle of Castle Rushen, recounting stories of medieval power struggles, to the intriguing Neolithic graves at Cashtal Ard.

1.2.4 Culinary Delights and Local Flavors: Take advantage of the chance to sample the delicious local cuisine of the Isle of Man, which is distinguished by its focus on fresh seafood, traditional Manx fare, and a blend of worldwide influences. Indulge in the island's gastronomic expertise in 2024 by visiting its quaint cafés, historic pubs, and elegant restaurants that highlight the finest of Manx cuisine.

1.2.5 Community and Cultural Immersion: 2024 offers a perfect opportunity to get fully immersed in the Isle of Man's strong community spirit thanks to its kind and inviting residents, who are renowned for their genuine hospitality. Participate in local celebrations, interact with the residents, and enjoy the friendly Manx hospitality to get a greater appreciation for the island's cultural diversity and to create relationships that go beyond simple distance.

Chapter 2: PLANNING YOUR TRIP

2.1 Entry Requirements and Visas

In terms of visa and entrance formalities, visiting the Isle of Man is generally not too complicated. The Isle of Man, a Crown Dependency of the UK, has its own immigration and visa laws that may somewhat diverge from those of the UK. A valid passport or national identification card is often adequate for admission for residents of the European Union and the European Economic Area (EEA). However, visitors from other nations should check with the relevant authorities or the British embassy or consulate in their area to confirm the precise admission requirements. It is essential to check that your travel papers are current and adhere to the standards established by the immigration officials in the Isle of Man.

2.2 Best Time To Visit

The Isle of Man provides a wide range of activities all year round, with each season having its special attraction. Tourists like to travel during the summer months of June through August because of the comfortable weather and lively atmosphere created by the many events and festivals. Outdoor activities, beach trips, and exploring the island's beautiful scenery are all perfect at this time.

The months of spring (March to May) and fall (September to November) are ideal for nature lovers and those looking for a more sedate getaway because of the great weather, fewer, and the island's countryside blossoming with vibrant flora. The Isle of Man has a peaceful allure in the winter (December to February) when it is possible to take crisp walks along lonely beaches and appreciate the island's calm beauty in a more private atmosphere.

2.3 Packing Tips

The moderate marine climate of the Isle of Man must be taken into account when you plan your journey there. No matter the season, it is a good idea to bring layers of clothes since the weather might change quickly. The most important items to pack are outerwear that is wind- and water-resistant, strong walking shoes for navigating the tough terrain, and cozy clothes appropriate for both active outdoor pursuits and strolls through charming towns.

It's also a good idea to bring sunscreen, sunglasses and a small umbrella or raincoat in case of unforeseen rains on the days that are more sunny. Don't forget to pack any required sports equipment, such as swimsuits, hiking boots, or cycle apparel, depending on your intended activities.

2.4 Options for Accommodation

The Isle of Man has a wide variety of lodging choices to accommodate different tastes and price ranges. There are accommodations for every kind of traveler on the island, from opulent hotels with breathtaking sea views to warm bed & breakfasts tucked away in the island's countryside.

The island offers a variety of upscale resorts and boutique hotels with top-notch facilities and individualized services for those wanting a hint of extravagance. As an alternative, travelers on a tighter budget might choose inexpensive guesthouses, self-catering flats, or classic Manx cottages, all of which provide a welcoming environment. Additionally, campers may make use of the picturesque campgrounds and RV parks on the island, which let them connect with nature and the great outdoors.

2.5 Getting Around

Numerous modes of transport make it easy to explore the Isle of Man, guaranteeing hassle-free travel across the island. The vast bus network, which connects most of the island's cities and villages, is among the most used types of transportation. The bus service provides a reliable, affordable way to move about. It runs regularly. Car rental options are easily accessible for those looking for additional freedom, enabling visitors to freely explore the island's nooks and crannies at their leisure. Cycling aficionados may also benefit from the island's bike-friendly paths and rent bicycles from a variety of rental shops. For individuals who want a more individualized and direct means of transportation, taxis and private rental services are also available. Last but not least, the Manx Electric Railway and the Isle of Man Steam Railway provide travelers with distinctive and nostalgic journeys across the island's breathtaking surroundings.

Chapter 3: ITINERARY FOR 2024

3.1 A 7-Day Schedule

Day 1: Arrival and Douglas Exploration

- **Morning**: Investigate Douglas, the nation's capital, and go to the Manx Museum to learn more about the history of the island.

- **Afternoon**: Take a leisurely walk down the lovely Douglas Promenade and stop at a neighborhood café for a typical Manx afternoon tea.

- **Evening**: Indulge in traditional Manx food at a nearby restaurant, savoring specialities, queens and the renowned Manx kippers.

Day 2: Views of the coast and castles

- **Morning** : Visit the famous Castle Rushen in the morning to take in its majestic medieval appearance and learn more about its fascinating history.
- **Afternoon** : Drive down the coast scenically in the afternoon, stopping at the charming Peel Castle for mesmerizing views of the Irish Sea.
- **Evening**: Savor a leisurely seafood supper at a restaurant on the water while admiring the setting sun.

Day 3: A Retreat into Nature

- **Morning** : Early in the morning, take a stroll through the lovely Glen Maye and take in the gushing waterfalls and verdant scenery.

- **Afternoon** : Explore the Calf of Man, a picturesque nature reserve filled with a variety of species and breathtaking coastline views, in the afternoon.
- **Evening**: Spend a cozy evening indulging in locally produced ales while taking in the peaceful atmosphere at a rural inn.

Day 4: A day of adventure

- **Morning**: Take part in thrilling outdoor sports like mountain biking along picturesque paths or sea kayaking along the island's rocky coastline.
- **Afternoon**: Try your hand at a game of golf at one of the island's top-notch courses, which have breathtaking scenery and difficult topography.

- **Evening**: Enjoy a substantial supper in a cozy setting while chatting with other intrepid travelers at a local bar.

Day 5: Cultural Tour

- **Morning**: Explore the historical treasures of the Manx Museum, which showcases the intriguing history of the island via a variety of exhibitions and artifacts.
- **Afternoon** : Visit the charming Rushen Abbey in the afternoon to take in the tranquil surroundings and learn more about the monastery's fascinating history.
- **Evening**: Attend an engaging folklore story and traditional music performance at a nearby theater to experience a cultural evening.

Day 6: Charms of the Sea

- **Morning:** Enjoy the peace and beauty of the island's natural beaches, such as Port Erin or Laxey Beach, while basking in the sun.
- **Afternoon**: Enjoy the breathtaking beauty and nostalgic allure of the island's ancient railroads by riding a historical steam train from Douglas to Port Erin.
- **Evening**: Savor a delectable seafood supper while watching the waves lazily wash the coast at a waterfront restaurant.

Day Seven: Final Exploration

- **Morning**: Take a stroll around the energetic hamlet of Laxey, which is renowned for its colorful mining past and spectacular Laxey Wheel, the biggest operational waterwheel on earth.

- **Afternoon**: Take a picturesque walk or ride the Snaefell Mountain Railway to the top of Snaefell, the island's tallest mountain, to take in the panoramic views.
- **Evening**: Say goodbye to the Isle of Man with a special farewell meal while reflecting on the magical experiences and making enduring travel memories.

3.2 A 14-Day Schedule

Days 1 through 7: Comply with the itinerary.

Day 8: Exploration of the North

- **Morning**: Travel to the island's north, stopping at the charming Point of Ayre and admiring the serene beauty of the northern shore.

- **Afternoon**: Take in a delicious lunch at a neighborhood restaurant while exploring the tiny hamlet of Ramsey, which is renowned for its picturesque harbor and ancient attractions.

- **Evening**: Take in the vibrant atmosphere of Ramsey's pubs and taverns while listening to live music and interacting with the welcoming people.

Day 9: A Culinary Adventure

- **Morning** : Visit a nearby farm or market in the morning to learn about Manx agriculture and enjoy fresh vegetables and handcrafted goods.

- **Afternoon**: Take part in a cooking class where you'll learn the techniques for making classic Manx cuisine from professional chefs.
- **Evening**: Indulge in a delicious meal that you prepared, complete with regional drinks and customary sweets.

Day 10: Coastal Adventures

- **Morning** : Explore the untamed western coastline in the morning, stopping at Niarbyl Bay to see the breathtaking sea cliffs and panoramic views.
- **Afternoon**: Visit one of the island's well-known surfing locations to partake in water sports like surfing or paddle boarding.
- **Evening**: Enjoy a beachside BBQ while toasting marshmallows and savoring

grilled treats while gazing up at the night sky.

Day 11: Immersion in art and culture

- **Morning** : Visit the dynamic House of Manannan in the morning, an engaging museum showcasing the island's illustrious maritime history and cultural heritage.
- **Afternoon**: Participate in an art class or gallery visit to learn more about the vibrant creative scene on the Isle of Man and to see the works of local artists.
- **Evening**: Attend a live music or cultural performance honoring the island's inventiveness and variety in the arts.

Day 12: Exploring the countryside

- **Morning**: Enjoy a leisurely horseback riding excursion around the lovely island countryside as you lose yourself in the peace of nature.

- **Afternoon**: Take a tranquil picnic in the middle of the beauty of nature while exploring the enthralling Ballaugh Curraghs, a protected wildlife area abounding with a variety of flora and animals.

- **Evening**: Relax with a spa treatment in a remote hideaway, rejuvenating your senses with holistic treatments and wellness rituals.

Day 13: Ancient Gardens and Trails

- **Morning**: Explore the Lhen Trench's historical heritage route to find old artifacts and archaeological sites tucked away in the lush terrain of the island.

- **Afternoon**: Take a stroll around the Milntown Estate and Gardens, taking in its well-kept lawns, colorful flower beds, and peaceful forests.
- **Evening**: Enjoy fine dining at a historic estate restaurant while taking in the atmosphere of a bygone age.

Day 14 : Goodbye and Reflection

- **Morning**: Enjoy one more leisurely walk around Castletown's quaint streets as you take in the town's rich history and magnificent architecture.
- **Afternoon**: Go souvenir shopping to pick up handmade goods, handcrafted items, and keepsakes to remember your fantastic vacation.
- **Evening**: Cherish the memories and encounters that have made your vacation unable to bid a heartfelt goodbye to the

Isle of Man with a reminiscence supper in a typical Manx bar.

3.3 Holidays and Festivals

Experience the thrilling Isle of Man TT Races, a famous motorcycle racing competition that draws fans and thrill-seekers from all over the world, from late May to early June. As you take in the exhilarating atmosphere and celebrate the spirit of racing, watch courageous racers negotiate the island's treacherous roads at fast speeds.

Take part in the celebrations of Tynwald Day, a historical event honoring the founding of the Isle of Man's parliamentary system, on July 5. Learn more about Manx history and government while taking in traditional music, dance, and cultural acts and seeing the ceremonial open-air session of the island's parliament.

Participate in Yn Chruinnaght (mid-July), a thriving international folk festival on the Isle of Man that honors the island's Celtic heritage. Enrich your connection to the island's cultural identity and creative spirit by taking in traditional music, dance, storytelling, and artisan displays.

Rushen Abbey's Mediaeval Fair (August): Relive the island's medieval past via reenactments, traditional crafts, and historical games at Rushen Abbey's Mediaeval Fair, an immersive experience. Experience the rich cultural and historical legacy of the Isle of Man while taking part in jousting competitions, medieval feasts, and artisan markets.

Chapter 4: MUST-SEE ATTRACTIONS

4.1 Douglas - The Capital

The Isle of Man's capital, Douglas, is tucked away along the east coast and charms tourists with its energetic vibe and variety of activities. The center of the city is the busy promenade, which provides panoramic views of the Irish Sea and is lined with a variety of stores and cafés. It is decorated with attractive Victorian architecture.

A lovely cultural experience is guaranteed at the Victorian marvel that is the Gaiety Theatre, which presents a range of acts from theater shows to musical concerts. The Manx Museum also provides a thorough overview of the history of the island by presenting artifacts and exhibits that highlight the Isle of Man's rich cultural heritage.

4.2 Castles and Heritage Locations

The Isle of Man is home to several castles and historic locations, all of which have something to do with the island's colorful past and provide tourists with a window into it. The Castle Rushen, a medieval fortification near Castletown that symbolizes the island's turbulent past and strategic importance, is one of the island's most recognisable sights.

The Peel Castle, perched impressively atop St. Patrick's Isle, offers breathtaking views of the nearby shoreline as well as a fascinating look into the island's Viking history. The captivating remains of the Hango Hill Viking Burial Site and the magnificent ancient tombs at Cashtal Ard, which show the Isle of Man's old Celtic heritage, are two other noteworthy historical locations.

4.3 Wonders of Nature

The stunning landscapes and varied ecosystems of the Isle of Man are shown by the island's natural treasures. For hikers and nature lovers, the island's highest summit, Snaefell Mountain, provides breathtaking panoramas of the Irish Sea and its lovely surroundings. The landmark Calf of Man, a natural reserve famed for its rich bird population and beautiful walking routes, is situated in The Sound, a region at the southern extremity of the island that mesmerizes tourists with its breathtaking coastline beauty. The picturesque Glen Maye and the striking Niarbyl Bay also highlight the island's craggy shoreline and provide the perfect locations for leisurely excursions and environmental discovery.

4.4 Historic Railroads

The Isle of Man is well known for its historic railroads, which provide tourists with a genuine and nostalgic opportunity to see the island's picturesque cities and breathtaking surroundings. The Victorian-era Isle of Man Steam Railway runs a charming route between Douglas and Port Erin through green scenery and lovely glens, offering travelers a gorgeous experience infused with old-world charm. Another famous historic mode of transport, the

Manx Electric Railway, connects Douglas with Laxey and Ramsey while offering passengers the chance to ride in antique trams and take in the breathtaking vistas of the island's eastern coast.

4.5 TT Competition and Racing

The Isle of Man TT (Tourist Trophy) Races, a famous yearly event that attracts motorcycle racing fans from all over the world, are a highlight for thrill-seekers and racing fanatics. The race, which is held on the island's difficult roads, features courageous riders who push the boundaries of speed and ability, generating an energizing mood that reverberates across the whole island. Witnessing the TT Races offers an unrivaled chance to feel the rush of racing against the breathtaking scenery of the Isle of

Man, making it a must-see for thrill-seekers and sports fans alike.

4.6 Galleries and Museums

A wide variety of museums and art galleries can be found on the Isle of Man, providing visitors with a thorough grasp of the island's cultural legacy and creative talent. In Peel, there is a museum called The House of Manannan that uses fascinating exhibits and immersive displays to bring the history and culture of the island to life. A look into the island's Victorian history is offered by Ramsey's Grove Museum of Victorian Living, which displays period-appropriate furniture and artifacts that illustrate everyday living at the time. A collection of modern works by national and international artists can be found at the Sayle Gallery in Douglas, which also fosters a lively artistic exchange and encourages creative expression within the island's cultural context.

Chapter 5: HIDDEN GEMS AND

OFF-THE-BEATEN-PATH

5.1 Remote Communities

The Isle of Man is home to outlying communities that capture the island's genuine beauty and tranquility and provide a retreat for anyone seeking a break from crowded tourist hotspots. An idyllic harbor view and a calm mood make Port St. Mary, which lies in the south, radiate a charming maritime character and are ideal for strolls along the shore. Through its well-preserved thatched huts and hands-on activities, the town of Cregneash, a living museum displaying ancient Manx crofting life, immerses visitors in the island's rich cultural history. Travelers are drawn to Maughold in the north by its rough coastline scenery, which includes remote beaches, old graveyards, and panoramic cliff-top vistas, guaranteeing an enchanted retreat into the island's untamed landscapes.

5.2 Beach Walks

The Isle of Man's gorgeous coastline offers a variety of spectacular walking paths, giving travelers the chance to fully appreciate the island's unadulterated natural beauty. A magnificent coastal trail known as the Raad ny

Foillan, or the Way of the Gull, circles the whole island and offers hikers breathtaking views, secret bays, and towering cliffs.

Adventurers are drawn to the Langness Peninsula, close to Castletown, for its scenic coastline hikes, possibilities for birding, and expansive vistas of the Irish Sea. From Port Erin to Port St. Mary, the Southern Headlands provide isolated beaches, amazing rock formations, and a variety of marine life, making it the perfect location for leisurely coastal exploration and nature enjoyment.

5.3 Dining and Local Cuisine

The cuisine of the Isle of Man is a combination of traditional and modern tastes, delivering a mouthwatering variety of regional specialities that highlight the island's illustrious culinary history. At one of the island's genuine eateries, indulge in the Loaghtan lamb, a treasured Manx delicacy famed for its juicy flavor and soft texture.

Try the famed Manx Queenies, ripe queen scallops plucked from the island's clear seas and masterfully cooked in a variety of culinary techniques that highlight their inherent sweetness and delicate flavor. A freshly caught kipper breakfast, cooked using traditional smoking techniques that give the fish a deep and distinctive flavor for a uniquely Manx dining experience, will give you a taste of the island's robust fishing sector.

5.4 Special Memorabilia

The Isle of Man has a wide selection of distinctive, regionally made keepsakes that make treasured keepsakes and capture the spirit of the island's natural and cultural splendor. Cozy blankets, cozy knitwear, and beautifully patterned textiles are just a few examples of handcrafted goods manufactured from the island's native Manx Loaghtan wool, which is famous for its softness and durability.

These things make excellent souvenirs or thoughtful presents. Enjoy locally prepared preserves and artisanal foods, such as mouth watering fruit jams, delicious handcrafted fudge, and traditional Manx chutneys, which highlight the island's dedication to quality and authenticity. Additionally, tourists have the opportunity to take home a piece of the meticulous workmanship and rich creative legacy of the Isle of Man by purchasing elaborate jewelry with Celtic influences made by talented local artists. These pieces serve as everlasting mementoes of guests' unforgettable trips to the Isle of Man.

5.5 Unique Places to Visit

The Isle of Man is home to a variety of oddball and outlandish attractions that give the island's varied offers a whimsical touch and provide unforgettable experiences that last with tourists long after they leave. The fabled and mysterious Fairy Bridge encourages visitors to make wishes as they pass by and adds to the enchanted and magical atmosphere of the island. Visitors get the opportunity to marvel at the Laxey Wheel, also known as Lady Isabella, which stands as a colossal architectural achievement and an homage to the island's industrial past. The Nautical Museum in Castletown offers a fascinating assortment of nautical artifacts and oddities, including an engaging exhibition on the island's unusual mermaid legend, which adds a touch of whimsy and marine folklore to the island's cultural tapestry.

Chapter 6: FREQUENTLY ASKED QUESTIONS

6.1 Banking and Money

- **Currency**: The Manx pound (IMP), which is equal to the British pound sterling (GBP), is the official unit of exchange for the Isle of Man. On the island, both currencies are commonly recognised, and major credit and debit cards are often used for purchases.

- **Banking Facilities**: The Isle of Man has a strong financial system, with several national and international institutions offering services including internet banking, currency exchange, and ATMs. To ease financial transactions throughout their stay, tourists may readily access banking services in major towns and cities.

6.2 Communication and Language

- **Language** : The official language of the Isle of Man is English, which is extensively used on the island. Manx Gaelic, an island-native Celtic language, is also seeing a revival as attempts are made to maintain and promote its use via cultural projects and educational activities.

- **Communication**: The Isle of Man is home to dependable internet and mobile phone coverage networks. Widespread coverage from major cell carriers ensures easy communication for both island inhabitants and visitors from elsewhere. Additionally, there are many public Fi hotspots in hotels, cafes and és, and spaces remaining connected while traveling.

6.3 Health and Safety

Travelers are said to feel comfortable when visiting the Isle of Man, which has low crime rates and a friendly local populace. However, it is recommended to take standard measures, such as protecting one's possessions and paying attention to one's surroundings, especially in busy places and popular tourist destinations.

- **Health**: The Isle of Man has a dependable healthcare system, comprising hospitals, clinics, and medical centers, guaranteeing that residents and tourists may receive high-quality healthcare services. Travelers are advised to bring any essential prescription medicine as well as a copy of any appropriate medical records, if applicable, and to get comprehensive travel insurance that covers medical emergencies.

6.4 Gratuities and Proper Conduct

- **Tipping**: Although not required on the Isle of Man, tipping is widely accepted. It is typical to tip between 10% and 15% of the entire bill at restaurants and cafés for excellent service. Tipping is appreciated but not required for other services like taxi rides and hotel help.

- **Etiquette**: It's crucial to follow local traditions and customs while visiting the Isle of Man. It is deemed courteous to use "please" and "thank you" in encounters and to greet individuals with respect and a warm demeanor. A pleasant and respectful interaction with the local people is fostered by being sensitive to cultural sensitivities and showing a sincere interest in the island's history and customs.

6.5 Connectivity and the Internet

- **Internet accessibility**: The Isle of Man has an internet connection, with Wi-Fi available in the majority of hotels, eateries, and public spaces. Additionally, several ISPs provide broadband services for locals and enterprises, guaranteeing a smooth online experience for both inhabitants and visitors.

- **Mobile Connectivity**: Travelers may use their mobile devices to remain connected thanks to the wide coverage that the island's major mobile network carriers offer. Visitors may also use international roaming services, which makes it easier for them to keep in touch while visiting the Isle of Man.

- **Public connection**: The Isle of Man has a strong infrastructure for public connection, with several internet cafés, open Wi-Fi hotspots, and libraries providing tourists with access to the internet. Additionally, the island's effective telecommunications network guarantees seamless connection for both personal and professional purposes, meeting the various demands of both visitors and locals.

Chapter 7: NEW UPDATES AND TRENDS FOR 2024

7.1. Upcoming Developments

In 2024, the Isle of Man will see several new construction and infrastructure projects aimed at improving the overall travel experience and fostering sustainable growth around the island. The introduction of electric car charging stations and increased accessibility for visitors to hire electric vehicles are two of the most eagerly awaited initiatives for the island's eco-friendly transportation system. Additionally, the building of dedicated bicycle pathways and the implementation of bike-sharing programmes would improve the cycling infrastructure, which will boost eco-friendly transportation and encourage residents and tourists to live better lifestyles.

The Isle of Man's tourist business is also embracing technology changes, implementing cutting-edge digital platforms and creating engaging visitor experiences to encourage personalized travel plans and provide easy access to information. The ongoing efforts to increase nature reserves, safeguard wildlife habitats, and promote eco-tourism activities that foster a deeper appreciation for the island's diverse ecosystems and natural wonders also reflect the island's commitment to protecting its natural heritage and promoting sustainable tourism practices.

7.2 Initiatives for Sustainable Travel

The Isle of Man is leading several sustainable travel projects to reduce the environmental impact of tourist operations and promote a more environmentally aware attitude to travel as part of its commitment to environmental protection and responsible tourism. The island is aggressively encouraging eco-friendly lodgings that follow sustainable practices, such as resource-conserving operations, waste management plans, and the usage of locally grown and organic goods. To recognise and reward companies that show a dedication to sustainability and eco-conscious operations, eco-certifications and green accreditation programmes are being created.

The Isle of Man places a strong focus on eco-friendly tourism, which includes its initiatives to support responsible outdoor recreation and nature-based learning opportunities that foster environmental awareness and conservation education. The island's various ecosystems and natural heritage are being preserved via eco-tours, guided nature hikes, and animal conservation programmes that offer tourists immersive experiences. Additionally, community-led sustainability initiatives and cooperative relationships with nearby conservation groups are building a shared commitment to preserving the Isle of Man's natural resources for future generations.

7.3 New Bars and Restaurants

In 2024, the Isle of Man's culinary scene will undergo a significant change as a result of the opening of a wide variety of new eateries and bars that will highlight the island's developing culinary scene and satisfy the many tastes and preferences of discriminating tourists. The Isle of Man's culinary offerings are experiencing a renaissance, embracing a fusion of international flavors and locally sourced ingredients to create a gastronomic journey that celebrates the island's rich culinary heritage.

These culinary offerings range from hip gastro pubs serving modern interpretations of traditional Manx dishes to chic fine dining establishments offering innovative culinary experiences.

In addition to the opening of new restaurants, the Isle of Man's thriving bar scene is also seeing the growth of speakeasies, craft brewers and artisanal cocktail bars that emphasize regionally made spirits and beers. These cutting-edge bars are distinguished by their focus on inventive mixology, custom cocktail menus, and immersive sampling experiences that provide customers with a unique insight into the Isle of Man's thriving beverage culture and developing craft beverage sector.

7.4 Options for Accommodation

In 2024, The Isle of Man will have a wider variety of lodging choices that will accommodate different traveler tastes and provide a seamless fusion of convenience, comfort, and immersive experiences. Luxury hotels and resorts are reshaping the island's hospitality scene by providing discriminating guests with a comfortable escape from the island's breathtaking natural settings. These properties are distinguished by their gorgeous décor and high-end services. These upscale lodgings place a high value on individualized services, carefully selected dining options, and luxurious wellness facilities to provide visitors seeking pleasure and relaxation with a sumptuous and revitalizing stay.

The Isle of Man's assortment of bed and breakfasts, guesthouses, and self-catering cottages offers a cozy and homely atmosphere for those looking for a more genuine and intimate experience, allowing guests to immerse themselves in the island's warm hospitality and embrace a customized approach to hospitality. For visitors looking for an authentic and immersive experience, these lodgings often include traditional Manx buildings and provide a true insight into the island's indigenous culture and community. The island's camping areas and glamping accommodations also appeal to outdoor adventurers and nature lovers, allowing a deeper connection to the island's pristine landscapes and a calm and tranquil atmosphere for travelers wanting a distinctive and nature-focused lodging experience.

Chapter 8: EXPLORATION IN 2024

8.1 Outdoor Recreation

For thrill-seekers and outdoor lovers, the Isle of Man has a wide range of thrilling adventure activities that allow for an immersive and adrenaline-fueled exploration of the island's rocky terrain and picturesque surroundings. The Isle of Man's adventure scene is bursting with chances for active exploration and pulse-pounding experiences, offering everything from exhilarating water sports like kayaking, paddleboarding, and coasteering along the island's picturesque coastline to exhilarating mountain biking and trail running adventures through the island's diverse terrain. For visitors looking to test their boundaries and go on remarkable outdoor adventures, the island's difficult rock-climbing locations, zip-lining courses, and adventure parks provide a dynamic and fascinating atmosphere.

8.2 Wildlife and Nature

There are several options for environment lovers and wildlife enthusiasts to immerse themselves in the island's intriguing biodiversity and gorgeous surroundings thanks to the Isle of Man's pristine natural landscapes and various ecosystems. The Ballaugh Curraghs and the Ayres National Natural Reserve, which exhibit a diverse diversity of flora and fauna and serve as a refuge for rare bird species and unique plant life, are just two of the captivating natural reserves on the island that tourists may visit. A closer look at the island's varied wildlife, including seals, dolphins, and migratory bird species, is also provided on guided nature walks, birdwatching tours, and wildlife-spotting excursions, making for memorable encounters and developing a deeper appreciation for the Isle of Man's natural wonders.

8.3 Exploring Neighborhood Islands

The Isle of Man is a perfect starting point for touring other islands and taking in the distinct character and attractiveness of the surrounding archipelago, in addition to its breathtaking scenery and cultural highlights. Visitors have the chance to explore the area's maritime history, natural beauty, and unique cultural attractions on day excursions to adjacent islands including the Isle of Man and the Calf of Man. Visitors may take boat trips and tour groups to these nearby islands where they can see their historical sites, charming towns, and stunning beaches while learning more about the maritime legacy and intertwined history of the surrounding isles.

8.4 Cultural Observations

A key component of exploration in 2024 will be immersing oneself in the Isle of Man's vibrant heritage and rich cultural tapestry, as the island continues to celebrate its distinctive customs, artistic endeavors, and historical legacy through a wide range of immersive experiences and cultural activities. The island's artistic talent and creative spirit are displayed in traditional folk music festivals, cultural workshops, and art exhibitions that visitors can attend. These events offer a firsthand look at the Manx cultural renaissance and help visitors gain a deeper understanding of the island's modern cultural landscape. Furthermore, cultural tours, heritage trails, and guided tours of historic sites like the Nautical Museum and Peel Castle provide an insightful exploration of the island's rich heritage and illustrious past, enabling visitors to follow in the footsteps of ancient civilizations and learn about the cultural quirks that define the Isle of Man's identity.

8.5 Entertainment and Nightlife

Travelers looking to relax, mingle, and savor the dynamic atmosphere and cultural offers of the Isle of Man may choose from a wide variety of activities thanks to the island's thriving nightlife and entertainment industry. The Isle of Man's entertainment venues cater to a wide range of preferences and offer a dynamic and engaging social environment for visitors to mingle with locals and other travelers. These venues range from lively pubs and traditional taverns hosting live music performances and cultural events to chic cocktail bars and modern lounges offering innovative mixology experiences and vibrant nightlife. Additionally, the island's energetic music festivals, theatrical productions, and cultural performances, held at numerous locations and event spaces all year long, highlight the artistic talent and creative vibrancy of the island, giving visitors the chance to experience the island's cultural diversity and exciting entertainment scene firsthand.

Chapter 9: TRAVEL RESOURCES

9.1 Useful Websites and Apps

- **Visit Isle of Man (Website):** The official tourist website of the Isle of Man offers thorough details about nearby landmarks, activities, lodgings, and travel advice, making it a useful tool for those planning their trip to the island.

- **Isle of Man Transport (App):** The Isle of Man Transport app provides easy access to the island's public transport timetables, routes and ticketing choices, enabling visitors to use the island's transport system quickly and effectively.

- **Isle of Man Weather (App):** By offering real-time weather updates, predictions, and warnings, the Isle of

Man Weather app enables visitors to keep informed about regional weather conditions and make appropriate plans for their outdoor activities.

- **Manx National Legacy (Website):** Offering visitors a thorough overview of the cultural attractions and educational resources available on the Isle of Man, the Manx National Heritage website provides insights into the island's rich cultural legacy, historical locations, and museum displays.

9.2 Transportation and Maps

- **Isle of Man Road Map**: A thorough road map of the Isle of Man is necessary for travelers navigating the island's scenic routes, coastal drives, and rural pathways because it gives a thorough overview of the topography of the island and makes it easier to explore its various landscapes and attractions.

- **Public Transportation Guide:** The complete public transportation guide for the Isle of Man provides details on bus timetables, routes, and prices, allowing visitors to conveniently move between the island's main cities and tourist destinations via a vast network of bus services.

- **Cycling Routes Map**: The Isle of Man's bicycle routes map shows designated cycling lanes, beautiful trails, and difficult terrain to accommodate outdoor explorers and cyclists looking to enjoy the island's attractive countryside and coastline panoramas on two wheels.

- **Ferry Timetable:** Having access to the ferry schedule is essential for travelers who want to schedule trips to adjacent islands and explore the archipelago. This will guarantee prompt departures and easy communication between the Isle of Man and its neighboring locations.

9.3 Travel Insurance

- **Comprehensive Coverage**: Choosing comprehensive travel insurance that includes coverage for medical emergencies, trip cancellations, and lost belongings offers travelers financial security and peace of mind while traveling to the Isle of Man, ensuring that unanticipated events do not interfere with their travel plans or jeopardize their health.

- **Emergency Assistance**: Travelers must make sure that their travel insurance policy includes 24-hour emergency assistance and repatriation services to ensure that they will receive prompt assistance and guidance in the event of unanticipated emergencies, medical emergencies, or travel delays while they are visiting the Isle of Man.

- **Policy Documentation:** Travellersrstantheir the specifics of their travel insurance policy, including coverage limits, exclusions, and claim procedures. This will help ensure a quick and easy claims process in the event of unforeseen incidents or emergencies requiring insurance coverage.

9.4 Checklist for Packing

Pack weather-appropriate attire to be prepared for the island's variable weather and a variety of outdoor activities throughout your stay. This includes waterproof outerwear, layers for different temperatures, and comfortable shoes.

- **Essential Travel Items**: The packing list should include all necessary supplies and provisions for a hassle-free and comfortable trip to the Isle of Man, including travel documents, identification, prescription medication, first-aid kits, and personal hygiene products.

- **Outdoor Gear**: Travelers who intend to explore the island's picturesque trails, coastal walks, and nature reserves must pack outdoor necessities like hiking gear, sun protection, insect repellent, and sturdy footwear for outdoor adventures and nature-focused activities without any inconvenience or discomfort.

9.5 Emergency Phone Numbers

Knowing the local emergency numbers is essential while visiting the Isle of Man to guarantee quick help in the case of unanticipated mishaps or crises. The following emergency numbers may help you be ready and handle any critical problems that could occur during your visit. Get familiar with them now.

- **Emergency Services**: To contact the police, fire department, or ambulance services immediately in the event of an emergency, phone 999, the emergency services number. The skilled emeSkilledonders are prepared to handle a variety of circumstances and provide individuals in need with prompt aid.

- **Medical Services**: Dial 999 to reach the Isle of Man's emergency medical services in the event of a medical emergency or the need for immediate medical assistance. First responders and devoted medical staff are skilled in providing emergency medical treatment, including ambulance services and quick transportation to the closest hospital for urgent care.

- **Consulate or Embassy**: Travelers are encouraged to always have the contact details of the local consulate or embassy on hand in case of any legal concerns, emergency scenarios involving documents, or circumstances needing diplomatic support. This guarantees that while you are visiting the Isle of Man, you will have access to consular services and advice from the diplomatic officials of your home country.

Learn how to reach local government offices, tourist information centers, and support services that can offer advice and assistance in situations other than emergencies, such as lost documents, travel-related questions, or general information about the island.

Keep your travel insurance provider's contact information handy so you can get in touch with them quickly if you experience any travel-related issues, such as the need for medical attention, delays in your trip plans, or missing luggage. Making contact with your insurance company guarantees prompt assistance and direction for handling any unanticipated difficulties throughout your vacation.

In addition to ensuring your safety and well-being, being proactive and aware of the required emergency contacts also brings peace of mind, enabling you to concentrate on taking advantage of the special experiences and attractions that the Isle of Man has to offer.

Chapter 10: CONCLUSION

10.1 Traveling Suggestions

Consider these crucial suggestions as you get ready to go to the Isle of Man to make your vacation unforgettable:

- **Embrace the Outdoors**: To truly appreciate the island's unspoiled beauty, take advantage of its spectacular natural sceneries and engage in outdoor activities like hiking, cycling, and coastline walks.

- **Engage with the Culture**: Discover the island's rich cultural legacy by taking part in regional celebrations, seeing historic locations, and appreciating local music and artwork. This will help you understand the Isle of Man's distinct cultural identity.

- **Taste Local Cuisine**: Indulge in the culinary pleasures of the island, from freshly caught fish to traditional Manx cuisine, and savor the flavors that capture the island's illustrious culinary history.

- **Connect with the Community**: Interact with the welcoming locals, strike up a discussion, and discover more about their way of life. The Manx people's warmth and friendliness are part of what makes the Isle of Man so charming.

- **Capture Memories:** Use your camera, a notepad, or a sketchbook to record the stunning scenery, exciting cultural activities, and special moments that make up your trip to the Isle of Man.

10.2 Leaving the Isle of Man with Fond Memories

Keep in mind the remarkable moments and encounters that have defined your adventure as you say goodbye to the Isle of Man:

- **Reflect on the Beauty**: Take a minute to consider the beauty of the island's stunning landscapes, serene seaside vistas, and enthralling natural treasures, which have made a lasting impression on your travels.

- **Recall Cultural Encounters**: Consider the enlightening cross-cultural encounters, neighborhood interactions, and immersion experiences that have given you a better understanding of the colorful Isle of Man history and customs.

- **Savour Culinary Delights:** Reminisce over the culinary explorations and gastronomic discoveries that have tantalize your taste buds and given you a greater knowledge of Manx culinary traditions as you savor the flavors and fragrances of the island's wonderful food.

- **Embrace Lasting relationships**: Treasure the friendships and relationships you make with friendly residents and other visitors, as these interactions and cultural exchanges can help you feel more at home and comradery throughout your time on the Isle of Man.

- **Plan Your Return:** Depart the Isle of Man with the comeo, discover its undiscovered attractions, take part in its lively festivals, and have more priceless experiences that will strengthen your bond with this alluring island.

In addition to signaling the conclusion of an amazing trip, leaving the Isle of Man with pleasant memories also heralds the beginning of a lifelong relationship with this magical island, urging you to return and rediscover its ageless charm and fascinating delights in the days to come.